Bugs That Live On Us

John Perritano

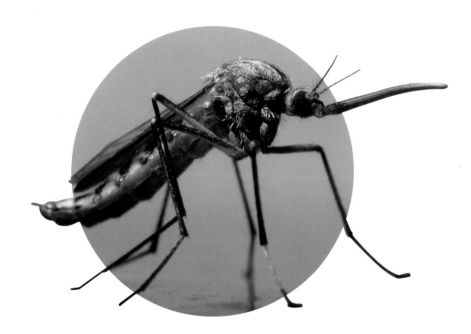

 **Marshall Cavendish**
Benchmark
New York

Marshall Cavendish Benchmark
99 White Plains Road
Tarrytown, NY 10591
www.marshallcavendish.us

Library of Congress Cataloging-in-Publication Data
Perritano, John.
   Bugs that live on us / by John Perritano.
      p. cm. -- (Bug alert)
   Includes bibliographical references and index.
   ISBN 978-0-7614-3187-9
1.   Parasitic insects--Juvenile literature. 2. Insects--Juvenile literature. I. Title.
   QL496.12.P47 2009
   595.717'857--dc22
   2008014595

The photographs in this book are used by permission and through the courtesy of:

Half Title : Göran Wassvik / Dreamstime
Sebastian Kaulitzki/ Shutterstock: P4; David Scharf/ Gettyimages: P5; Eye of science / Science Photo Library: P7;
John Cooke /Oxford Scientific (OSF)/ Photolibrary:P9; AJ Photo/ SPL/ Photolibrary: P11, David mack / Science
Photo Library: P12tr; Eye of science / Science Photo Library: P13; Steve Gschneissner/ SPL/ Photolibrary: P15;
Yury Maryunin/ Dreamstime:P17; Oxford Scientific (OSF)/ Photolibrary: P19;
Andrew Syred/ Science Photo Library: P21; K Wothe/ Picture Press/ Photolibrary: P23;
Göran Wassvik / Dreamstime: P25; Kage Manfred P/ Oxford Scientific (OSF)/
Photolibrary: P27; Sleepy Weasel Entertainment/ Istockphoto: P28; Kim Taylor/ Naturepl.
Cover photo: Eye Of Science / Science Photo Library

Illustrations : Q2A Media Art bank.

Created by: Q2A Media

Creative Director: Simmi Sikka

Series Editor: Maura Christopher

Series Art Director: Sudakshina Basu

Series Designers: Mansi Mittal, Rati Mathur and Shruti Bahl

Series Illustrators: Indranil Ganguly, Rishi Bhardwaj, Kusum Kala and Pooja Shukla

Photo research by Anju Pathak

Series Project Managers: Ravneet Kaur and Shekhar Kapur

Printed in Malaysia

135642

Contents

Big, Bad Bugs!

They could be in your bed! They could be in your hair! They might even be crawling on you—or in you—this very second. Some feed on warm blood. Others feed on dead skin. Some will make you itch. Others will make you cringe. You might not know it, but your body could be a bug hotel for mites, lice, and bedbugs. They are waiting to crawl into your ears, burrow into your skin, or bite you while you sleep.

Here Come the Parasites

These nasty creatures are *parasites*. Parasites are **organisms** that live on or in another living being, such as a human or an animal. *Endoparasites* are parasites that live inside people and animals, such as tapeworms. *Ectoparasites* are parasites that live on an animal's or person's body. Lice and fleas are ectoparasites.

Scratch Time

The itch mite can get on a human's skin if the person rubs up against grass or leaves. You might not be able to see an itch mite or feel it when it bites. But as its name suggests, the itch mite wil irritate your skin and make you—itch.

Mighty Mite

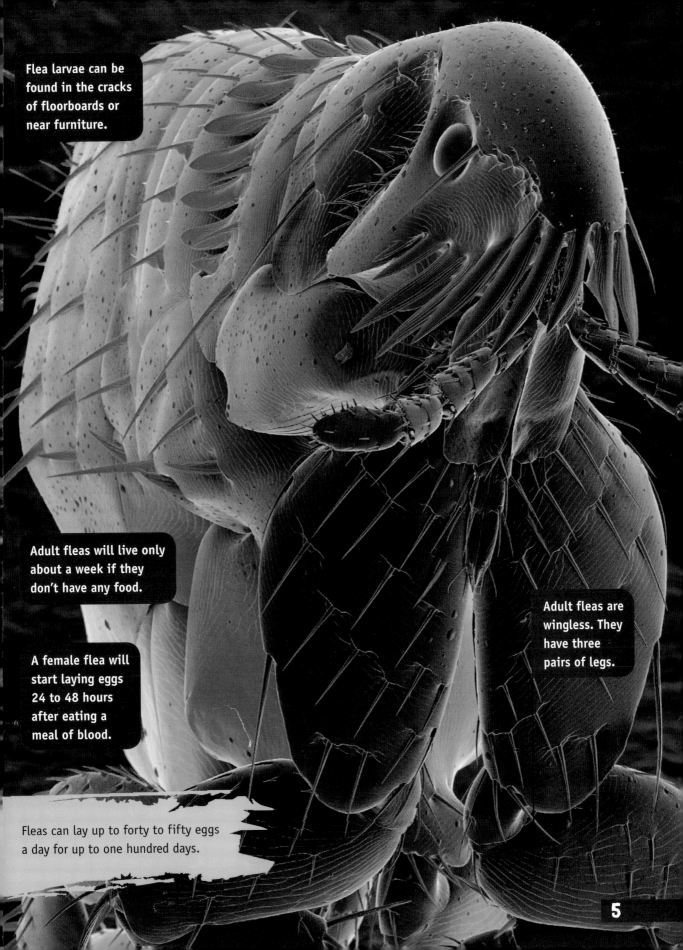

Flea larvae can be found in the cracks of floorboards or near furniture.

Adult fleas will live only about a week if they don't have any food.

A female flea will start laying eggs 24 to 48 hours after eating a meal of blood.

Adult fleas are wingless. They have three pairs of legs.

Fleas can lay up to forty to fifty eggs a day for up to one hundred days.

Dinner Is Served

Like all living creatures, parasitic insects need food to live. Humans just happen to be on the menu.

Come and Get 'Em

According to one study, about 1.5 billion people, or slightly more than 25 percent of the world's population, have roundworms. More than 1.3 billion people carry hookworms in their small **intestines** where food is digested. Body lice cause many people to scratch themselves constantly. Body lice lay their eggs in the seams of clothing or on bedding. Unlike head lice, body lice can transmit diseases, such as **typhus.** The most serious form of typhus can affect people's brains, lungs, and kidneys.

One for the Books

Everyone loves a world record. But for a woman named Sally Mae Wallace, it was a dubious honor to have the world's longest tapeworm removed from a human body. Doctors pulled a 37-foot tapeworm out of Sally Mae's gut in 1991.

Tale of the Tape

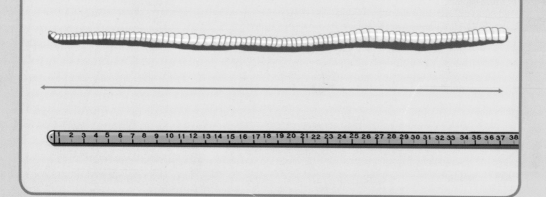

The female will burrow into the skin of its host. As it feeds under the skin, the flea will leave the tip of its abdomen out so it can breathe.

The Chigoe flea is the tiniest flea around.

Two weeks after burrowing under the skin, the Chigoe flea will lay its eggs. Those eggs will hatch within four weeks.

The Chigoe flea lives in sand and in soil.

The Chigoe flea attacks bare feet. This pest will burrow into the skin. Often, doctors have to remove the flea surgically.

Head Lice

In 2005, an entire school in New Jersey had to close for a time because the heads of its students were infested with head lice. In Great Britain, head lice infestations have increased so much that nearly half of all eleven-year-olds are infested each year with these pests.

▲ Head lice can jump from head to head.

What Are They?

Head lice are gray, wingless creatures about .07 inches (2 millimeters) long. They thrive close to the scalp. People get head lice from sharing infested clothing, such as scarves, hats, and coats. Head lice need warm, human blood to survive. Adult lice will die in two days if they have nothing to eat.

Life Cycle

1. Nits are head lice eggs. They are tiny—no bigger than a knot at the end of a fine piece of thread. Adult females lay nits near the scalp where they attach tightly to a shaft of hair.
2. The nit hatches into an infant louse called a **nymph**.
3. Baby nymphs become adults in seven days. They feed on human blood.
4. The adult louse is about the size of a sesame seed. Adult lice can live for thirty days on a person's head.

Life Cycle

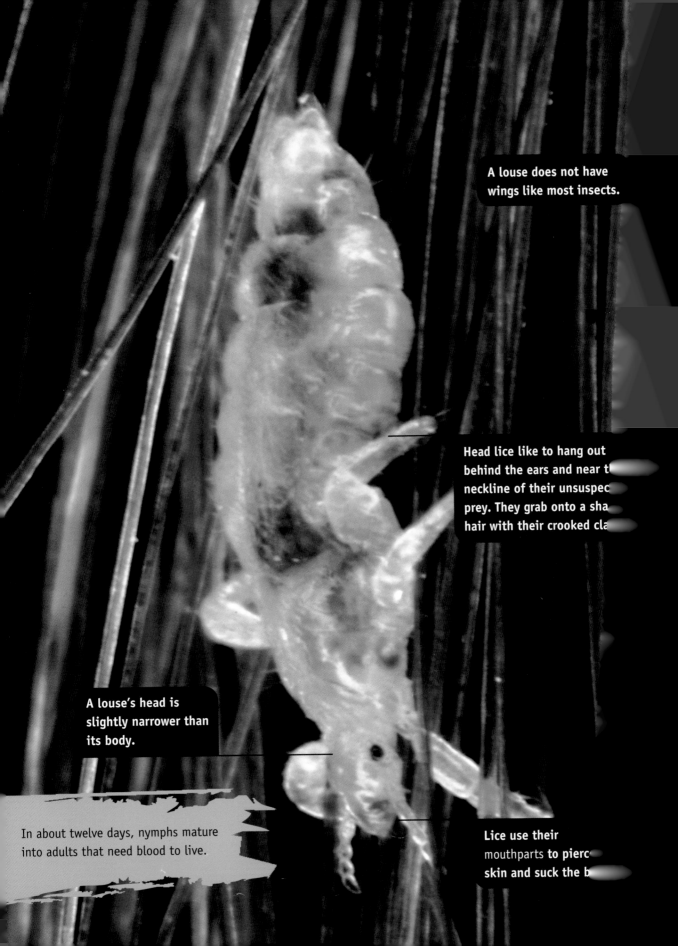

A louse does not have wings like most insects.

Head lice like to hang out behind the ears and near t[he] neckline of their unsuspec[ting] prey. They grab onto a sha[ft of] hair with their crooked cla[ws].

A louse's head is slightly narrower than its body.

In about twelve days, nymphs mature into adults that need blood to live.

Lice use their mouthparts **to pierc**[e] skin and suck the b[lood].

Treating Head Lice

Head lice are very common in schools. To combat these annoying creatures, doctors recommend using a pediculicide (peh-DICK-you-luh-side). This medicine will kill the vermin, but it might have to be applied more than once to destroy all the nits. Other ways to combat the spread of head lice include:

▲ Head lice can cause sores on the head that may become infected.

- Soaking combs and brushes in rubbing alcohol for one hour or washing them in hot water and soap
- Vacuuming the floor and furniture
- Completely avoiding head-to-head contact with anyone
- Not sharing combs, brushes, hats, and towels
- Washing sheets and bedspreads in hot water.

Hangers On

Head lice are generally found on the scalp, behind or near the ears. They hang on with their claws. You will rarely find head lice on your body, eyelashes, or eyebrows.

Nit-picking

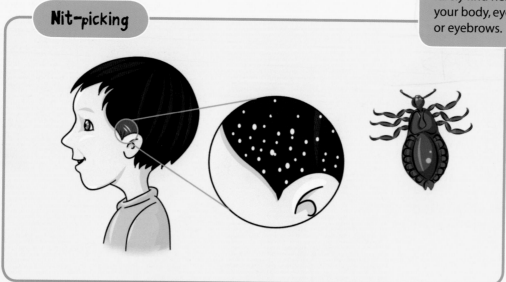

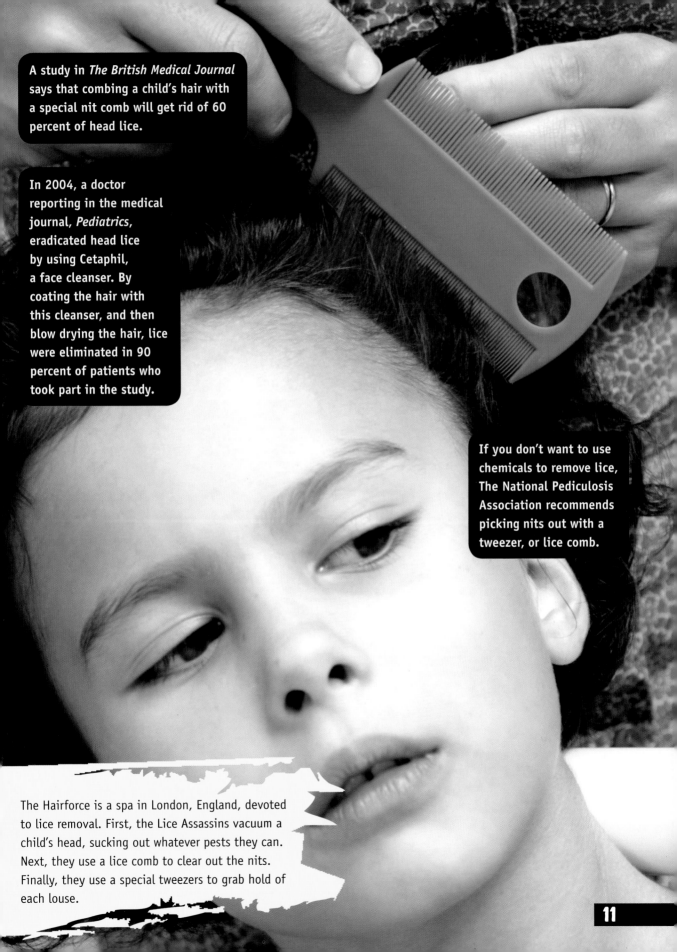

A study in *The British Medical Journal* says that combing a child's hair with a special nit comb will get rid of 60 percent of head lice.

In 2004, a doctor reporting in the medical journal, *Pediatrics*, eradicated head lice by using Cetaphil, a face cleanser. By coating the hair with this cleanser, and then blow drying the hair, lice were eliminated in 90 percent of patients who took part in the study.

If you don't want to use chemicals to remove lice, The National Pediculosis Association recommends picking nits out with a tweezer, or lice comb.

The Hairforce is a spa in London, England, devoted to lice removal. First, the Lice Assassins vacuum a child's head, sucking out whatever pests they can. Next, they use a lice comb to clear out the nits. Finally, they use a special tweezers to grab hold of each louse.

Tapeworms

Tapeworms are one of the largest parasites that live inside people.

What Are They?

Tapeworms are long, flat worms that live in the intestines of humans and many other animals. Usually humans ingest the organism by eating food or water containing tapeworm eggs or **larvae**. If you have a tapeworm, your stomach hurts, you feel like vomiting, and you have diarrhea.

Many Sections

The body of the tapeworm is made up of many segments. Each segment contains thousands of eggs. These segments join behind the tapeworm's head, making it longer and longer.

▲ Tapeworms spend most of their lives in the tissue of one or more animals.

Life Cycle

1. An adult tapeworm lays millions of eggs.
2. Animals eat plants covered with those eggs.
3. The eggs hatch into larvae, which move into the animal's muscles.
4. A person eats meat from the animal and is infected with the larvae in the capsules.
5. After several months, adult tapeworms emerge and grow inside the person.

Life Cycle

The worm's neck region is made up of a series of flat, rectangular body segments. These segments are known as proglottids (proe-GLAH-tuds).

A tapeworm has a knoblike head, or a scolex. The scolex is equipped with hooks for attaching to its prey's intestines.

Since a tapeworm does not have a mouth, it absorbs food through its body.

Tapeworms feed on digested food.

Sometimes the proglottids break apart. The worm's host then defecates and passes the bits of tapeworm out of its body. If the worm's scolex and neck are still whole, however, the worm is alive and can still grow.

The beef tapeworm is most commonly found in the United States.

13

Threadworms

People develop a threadworm infection when they inhale or swallow threadworm eggs. If the eggs are inhaled, they make their way into the lungs and eventually into a person's throat.

What Are They?

Also known as pinworms, threadworms are small, thin worms that make their home in the **rectum** of humans. The threadworm looks like a piece of fine cotton thread.

Easy to Spread

Threadworms are highly contagious. Their eggs can travel on dust, clothing, bedding, or toys. Sharing these items spreads the infection. Humans are the only living things that can get threadworms, although the eggs might stick to an animal's fur. It is important to wash your hands after touching a dog or cat that has been outside so threadworm eggs cannot be transferred to your body.

▲ Threadworms can infect children and adults.

Life Cycle

1. Once the eggs are inside the throat, the person unknowingly swallows them.
2. Within days, those eggs enter the **digestive system**.
3. The eggs mature and hatch into worms.
4. The female worm lays eggs on the human rectum.

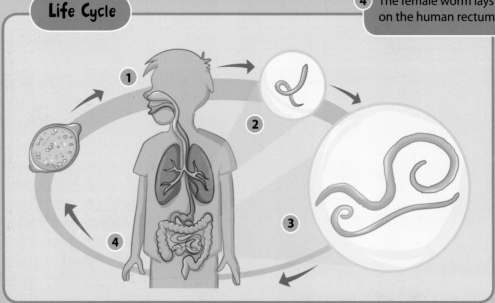

Life Cycle

The head of the worm has three small lips.

The adult pinworm male is 4/100 to 1/10 inches (1 to 4 mm) long. The female can be 1/3 to 1/2 inches (8 to 13 mm) long.

Its curved tail contains a small, fluid-filled sac that reduces friction when the worm moves.

The area around where the female has laid eggs will itch. When scratched, the tiny eggs cling to a person's fingers. Once on a person's fingers, the eggs can move to other areas, such as tables, food, liquids, or other people.

Those who suffer from a threadworm infection might itch violently at night, making it difficult to sleep.

Human Botflies

Found in Central and South America, the human botfly produces larvae that can really crawl out of your skin! They do that without even biting you themselves. They use mosquitoes to deliver their eggs, which hatch into larvae, or maggots, inside humans. Some people who have been bitten by a hairy botfly say they can feel the maggots moving under their skin.

◄ Botflies can be found on tropical fruit and vegetables.

What Are They?
The human botfly is an insect. Adults are roughly 5/10 to 7/10 inches (12 to 18 mm) long and slightly blue. They look a bit like bumblebees.

On and Under the Skin
While on a person's skin, the maggots eat their way deep into his or her muscle. Little hooks hold the maggots in place. They breathe by leaving a hole in the flesh.

Life Cycle
1 The female botfly attaches her eggs to a mosquito.
2 When that mosquito bites a human, the botfly's eggs are also injected.
3 The person's body heat causes the botfly eggs to hatch. Larvae emerge and burrow into the person, causing a small wound.
4 After six weeks, the maggots eat their way out of the body and drop to the ground.
5 On the ground, the maggots pupate, or transform themselves within a protective cocoon.
6 In twenty days, adult botflies fly away.

Life Cycle

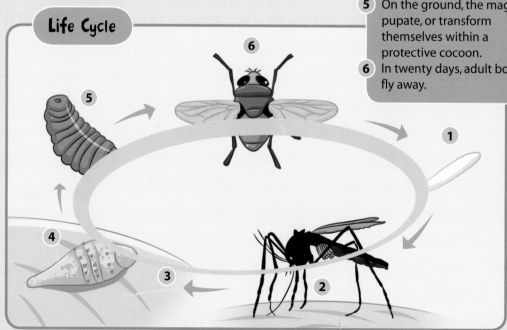

Botflies have three simple eyes and a pair of compound eyes. **The eyes on male botflies are closer together than the females' eyes.**

Like most flies, the botfly has three body regions: the head, the thorax, **and the** abdomen.

Botflies also attack livestock, such as sheep and horses. The sheep botfly lay eggs in the nostrils of the animal.

The fly breathes through tiny holes in its abdomen.

The insect's legs and wings are attached to its thorax.

Duct tape over a botfly wound will cut off the botfly's air supply, killing the bug.

Bedbugs

"Good night, sleep tight, don't let the bedbugs bite," goes the old saying. Well, bedbugs do bite, and the problem has been getting worse in recent years, especially in the United States. The number of complaints about bedbug infestations has soared in the last five years.

▲ Bedbugs are found in all countries.

What Are They?

Bedbugs are reddish-brown pests. They grow to only about 1/5 inches (0.5 centimeters) long. Bedbugs drink blood and bite people when they are sleeping.

World Travelers

Experts say the bugs are stowing away in the luggage of international travelers. They bring the bugs in from other countries. The bugs are now popping up everywhere. You can find them in expensive hotel rooms or in college **dormitories**.

Life Cycle

1. Female bedbugs lay their eggs in the nooks, crannies, cracks, and crevices of floorboards or in beds.
2. The eggs hatch in one or two weeks.
3. Newly hatched nymphs begin feeding immediately.
4. The newly hatched bugs remain as nymphs for two to four weeks. They will shed their skin several times before becoming adults.

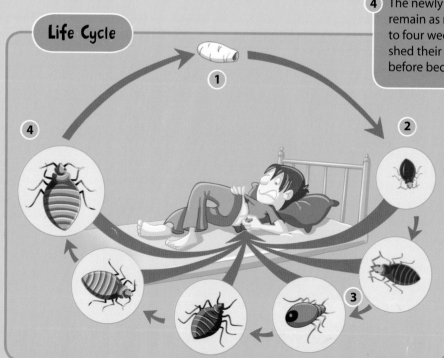

Life Cycle

Usually bedbugs will dine at night, but they will eat during the day when the light is dim.

Bedbugs pierce the skin of unsuspecting sleepers with their long beaks. They use their beaks like straws to suck up blood.

Bedbugs have very short forewings and no hind wings.

Bedbugs will leave tiny, bloody wounds after they feed. If you're bitten when you sleep, you might notice tiny spots of blood on the sheets.

Dust Mites

Did you know that you could be sharing your bed with 100,000 to 10 million dust mites? Each mite can produce twenty waste droppings each day. Many people are allergic to those droppings. Some people even get asthma because of them. Asthma is a disease of the respiratory system, in which the airways are inflamed or swollen.

▲ Watery eyes, a runny nose, sneezing and itching might be symptons of a dust-mite allergy.

What Are They?

Dust mites are **arachnids**. These **microscopic** monsters feast on dead skin cells. Humans shed about 1/5 of an ounce (6 grams) of dead skin each week. A typical mattress might contain thousands of dust mites. They feed on these human sheddings. Nearly 120,000 dust mites can live on one square yard (100,000 on 1 square meter) of carpet.

Sweet Dreams

Generally, dust mites live in bedding and thrive in warm, humid environments. They do not like icy temperatures.

Roommates!

Skin Feast

Female dust mites can lay up to eighty eggs at a time. It takes about one month for an egg to mature into an adult.

While you can definitely see a dust mite under a microscope, you might be able to see it with a magnifying glass.

Dust mites need at least 70 percent humidity to survive.

Dust mites have eight hairy legs, no eyes, and **no** antennae.

Male and female dust mites are round and often creamy white. They also have a striped cuticle, the tough outer layer of the organism.

Washing your sheets in water that is 130 degrees Fahrenheit (54 Celsius) will kill dust mites.

Ticks

▲ Ticks are arachnids.

The woods and people's backyards are teaming with ticks. They wait in fields of grass, among the leaves of trees, or near the tomato plants in the garden. They want to feed—on blood.

What Are They?

Ticks are not insects but arachnids like spiders and scorpions. Arachnids have four pairs of legs and no antenna. Ticks cannot fly. They can only crawl. If you find a tick on the back of your neck, chances are it walked across your body to get there.

Spreading Disease

Some ticks cause diseases such as Rocky Mountain spotted fever and Lyme disease, an illness common in the northeaster United States. Lyme disease will often mimic the flu. Doctors treat Lyme disease with a group of drugs called antibiotics. Antibiotics kill the growth of bacteria that can cause disease.

1 American Dog Tick

Also known as the wood tick, the American dog tick's larvae and nymphs feed on small animals. Adults feed on larger mammals, including humans and dogs.

2 Deer Tick

Deer ticks are responsible for transmitting Lyme disease. Once the deer tick's eggs hatch in the spring, the larvae will feed on small mammals, such as mice.

3 Brown Dog Tick

The brown dog tick feeds on dogs but rarely bites people. It can survive indoors.

Life Cycle

1

2

3

Ticks have two chelicerae near the mouth. The chelicera cuts through the skin of its prey.

When a tick eats, its body, or idiosoma, gets larger as the bug fills with blood.

Adult ticks have eight legs. Each leg is covered with short hairs. Each leg has a tiny claw at the end.

Ticks will latch onto their unsuspecting host when an animal or human brushes past.

Mosquitoes

You have swatted them. You have scratched their bites. They are the bugs that can turn any midsummer night's dream into a nightmare. Worldwide, mosquitoes kill more people than any other single factor. In the United States, mosquitoes spread diseases such as West Nile virus and encephalitis (in-seh-fuh-LIE-tess).

▲ Mosquitoes don't see well.

What Are They?

Like most insects, a mosquito's body consists of a head, a thorax, and an abdomen. The female has a **proboscis**. The insect uses its proboscis to pierce the skin of its dinner and sucks its blood.

Attack of the Mosquito

Mosquitoes have been around for 30 million years. They are experts at finding people to prey on. Mosquitoes can detect the chemicals that you exhale and the warmth of your body. Clothes of certain colors will also attract mosquitoes.

Streamlined Danger

1. The bug's two wings and six legs attach to the thorax.
2. The heart and the muscles the insect needs to fly are also in the thorax.
3. The abdomen contains the bug's digestive system.
4. The head contains all the equipment the mosquito needs to find you, including the bug's compound eyes, antennae that sense chemicals, a mouth, and a proboscis.

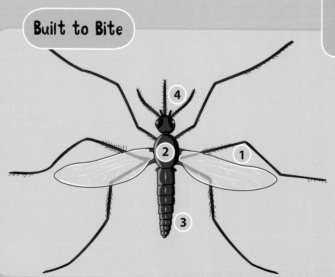

Built to Bite

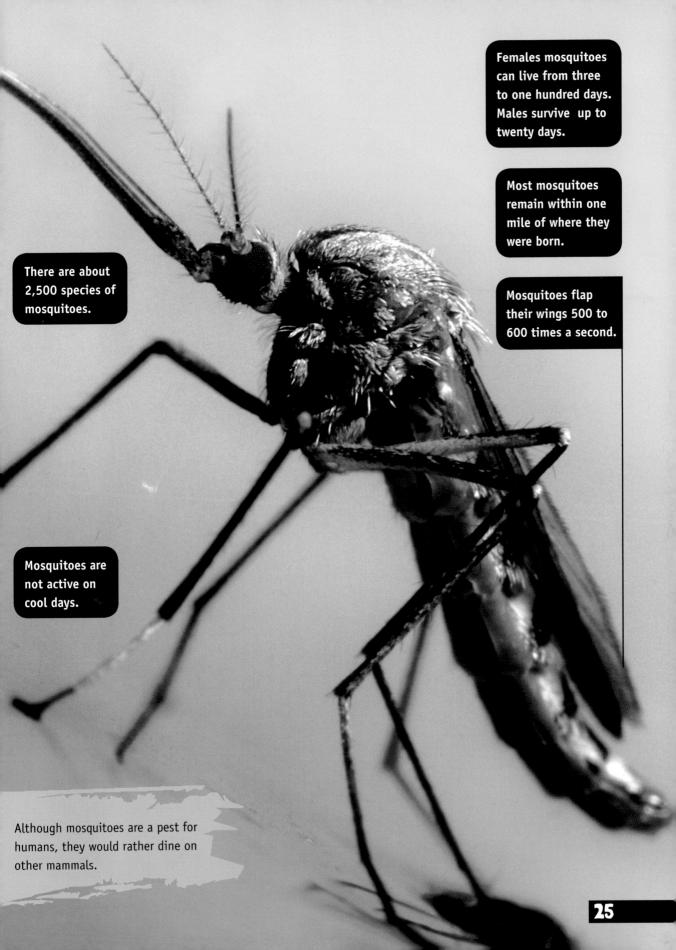

Females mosquitoes can live from three to one hundred days. Males survive up to twenty days.

Most mosquitoes remain within one mile of where they were born.

There are about 2,500 species of mosquitoes.

Mosquitoes flap their wings 500 to 600 times a second.

Mosquitoes are not active on cool days.

Although mosquitoes are a pest for humans, they would rather dine on other mammals.

Fleas

Perhaps you have seen a dog scratch its neck, or a cat bite its coat. When you look closer, you notice the animal has fleas. Suddenly, one flea jumps on you. It can jump more than two hundred times its own body length. That is like a human leaping over the top of the Empire State Building in New York City.

▲ Fleas have flat bodies and six strong legs for jumping.

What Are They?

A kind of insect, fleas have three pairs of legs and no wings. Fleas are tiny, only 1/16 to 1/8 inches (1.5 to 3.3 mm) long. Their bodies are flat on each side, allowing them to slide easily between the hairs on their hosts' bodies. As adults, they feed on the blood of cats, dogs, and people. As larvae, they feed on food droppings, flakes of dead skin, and other material from animals.

Life Cycle

1 The female flea can lay as many as 400 eggs.
2 Eggs hatch into larvae.
3 In the **pupae** stage, the larvae make little cocoons.
4 In seven to ten days, adult fleas emerge from the cocoon.

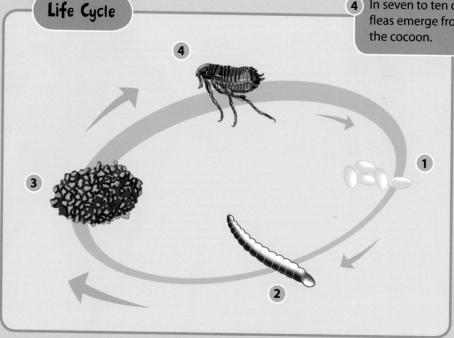

Life Cycle

A flea's antennae are sensitive and can detect the slightest movement of an approaching animal.

Fleas can jump so high because their long back legs are like springs. When they want to jump, they release their "spring" and shoot into the air.

Fleas can make an animal scratch so much that the animal will lose its hair.

Fleas can eat approximately fifteen times their body weight.

A Houseful of Bugs

Now that you know which bugs live in you and on you, it is time to find out which bugs live with you. You will find some of them crawling around your floor or just outside your house. You might be sitting near some right now.

Silverfish

The silverfish is another bug that likes to call your house its home. Silverfish live in wallpaper, old books, and the kitchen sink. Silverfish do not have wings and are pale gray. Thin scales cover their bodies.

Termites

Perhaps no bug is as destructive as a termite. Termites are tiny wood-eating bugs that can cause serious damage to houses and buildings. Americans spend more than $2 billion each year to control termites.

Now that you've read about some of the parasitic bugs in the world, remember: sleep tight, and don't let the bedbugs—or any other bugs—bite.

Cockroaches

No bug has been around longer than thecockroach. The earliest cockroach **fossils** show that they lived between 354 to 295 million years ago. That means the bugs survived when the dinosaurs became **extinct** some 65 million years ago. Cockroaches live in a variety of environments but prefer warm areas of buildings. Most cockroaches are **nocturnal** and will wake up when you turn on the lights.

Home Alone?

Silverfish like to run quickly. They are most active at night.

Adults can be as long as 3/4 of an inch long.

Some silverfish can live as long as eight years.

Silverfish can go for a year without eating.

Silverfish have long tails and two long antennae. They like to chew things and will dine on flour, oats, and glue.

Bug Data

Books

Davies, Nicola. *What's Eating You?*: Parasites—*The Inside Story*. Cambridge, MA: Candlewick Press, 2007.

Fleisher, Paul. *Parasites: Latching on to a Free Lunch*. Minneapolis, MN: Twenty-First Century Books, 2006.

Royston, Angela. *Head Lice* (It's Catching). Chicago: Heinemann Library, 2002.

Tilden, Thomasine. *Belly-Busting Worm Invasions!: Parasites That Love Your Insides*. New York: Scholastic Library Publishing, 2007.

Internet Sites

Visit these Web sites for more information:

Enchanted Learning
http://www.enchantedlearning.com/subjects/insects/mosquito/lifecycle.shtml

MSNBC
http://www.msnbc.msn.com/id/11916682/

Headlice.org
http://www.headlice.org/kids/

Glossary

abdomen: The region of the body that is farthest back in insects and arachnids.

antenna (plural: antennae): A feeler located on the head of insects and other bugs.

arachnid: A class of animals that includes spiders, scorpions, mites, and ticks. They have segmented bodies that are divided into two regions and eight legs.

compound eyes: Eyes made up of a number of separate lenses.

digestive system: The various body organs that are responsible for digesting food.

dormitory: A large building often on a college campus with a number of rooms for students to live in.

extinct: To die out completely.

fossil: The remains of an ancient plant or animal preserved in rock.

host: An animal that provides food for a parasite, an organism that lives on or in that animal.

intestines: Parts of the body through which food passes after it is eaten and leaves the stomach and where nutrients and water from digested food are absorbed and waste products solidify into feces.

larva (plural: larvae): The immature form of an insect; a larva often looks likea worm.

maggot: the legless, wormlike larva of a fly.

microscopic: Describes something so small that it can only be seen under a microscope.

mouthpart: Body part near the mouth used for gathering or eating food.

nocturnal: Most active at night.

nymph: An immature form of an insect. Nymphs are usually more developed than larvae.

organism: A living creature.

proboscis: A long body part shaped like a tube near the mouth of an invertebrate.

pupa (plural: pupae): A cocoonlike resting form of an insect; the insect changes from an immature form to an adult form inside the pupa.

rectum: A portion of the large intestine.

thorax: The part of an insect's body between the head and abdomen.Wings and legs are part of the thorax.

typhus: A disease with a high fever often transmitted by mites, fleas, and lice.

Index